MODERN K

ABC...
WHAT AN
INFORMED

VOTER

YOU'LL
BE!

ILLUSTRATED BY **JACY CORRAL**

A stands for

Affirmative Action

In 1961, we gave more rights to all people and pushed forward a positive reaction.

B stands for

Bicameral Legislature

Since 1789, our lawmaking body of two chambers, makes decisions and laws for our people and nature.

C stands for

Constitution

...our supreme law of the land. This document provides justice, tranquility, and rights to you and me, and will forever stand.

D stands for

Democracy

...or government by the people, you and me.

E stands for

Electoral College

Since our Constitution, these elected people vote to decide our President and Vice President to the best of their knowledge.

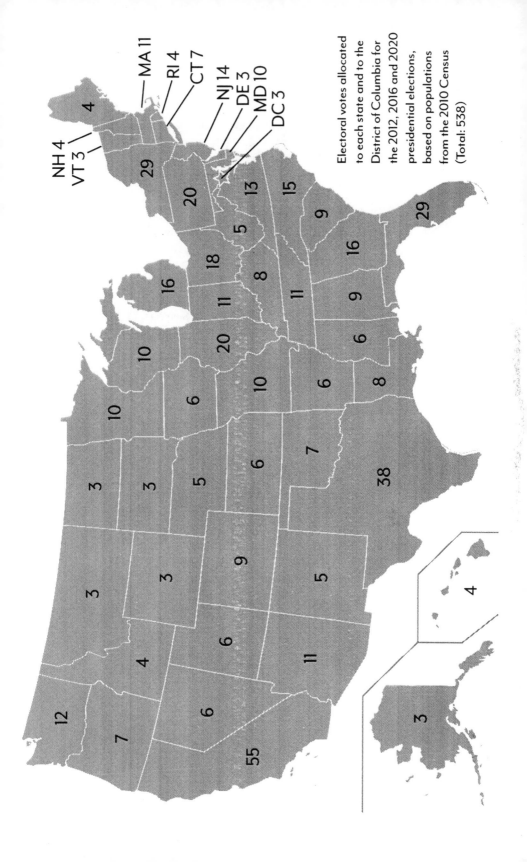

NH 4
VT 3
MA 11
RI 4
CT 7
NJ 14
DE 3
MD 10
DC 3

4
29
20
5
13
15
16
9
29
18
16
8
11
11
9
6
10
20
10
6
8
10
6
6
7
10
3
3
5
6
38
3
3
9
5
4
6
11
12
7
6
55

3
4

Electoral votes allocated
to each state and to the
District of Columbia for
the 2012, 2016 and 2020
presidential elections,
based on populations
from the 2010 Census
(Total: 538)

F stands for

First Amendment

...or freedom of the press, religion, and speech. To every individual, this civil liberty will reach.

General Election

In our country, on a Tuesday in November, we vote for the leaders of our country to lead us in our desired direction.

H stands for

House of Representatives

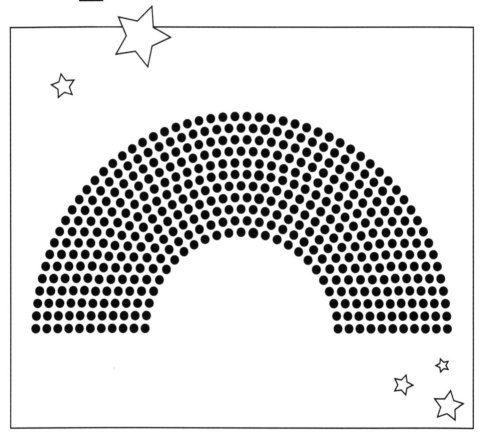

...which now has 435 people. Since 1789, they have met to help make laws for our country at the Capitol as our congresspeople.

I stands for

Individual Rights

...or Amendments one to ten.
These Bill of Rights give the power
to the people, once again, AMEN!

J stands for

Judicial Review

This power gives the Supreme Court the power to check that our laws are consistent for all the people of today, including you!

K stands for

John F. Kennedy

He was the youngest elected President in
our history, asking the nation "what you
can do for your country" and its identity.

L stands for

Law

These rules govern all of us. They begin as a bill in Congress that lawmakers must then discuss.

M stands for

Martin Luther King, Jr.

He was a social activist during the Civil Rights Movement, who urged the people to "let freedom ring".

Nineteenth Amendment

...or the right to vote for women. It started in 1919, and has brought thousands of women into elections since then.

O stands for

Oval Office

...the President's office in the White House.
It is in the West Wing of the house, the
opposite wing of their spouse.

P stands for

President

...the head of the state. The President directs the executive branch, and is our commander in chief. We've had 45 Presidents in the US to date.

Q stands for

Quorum

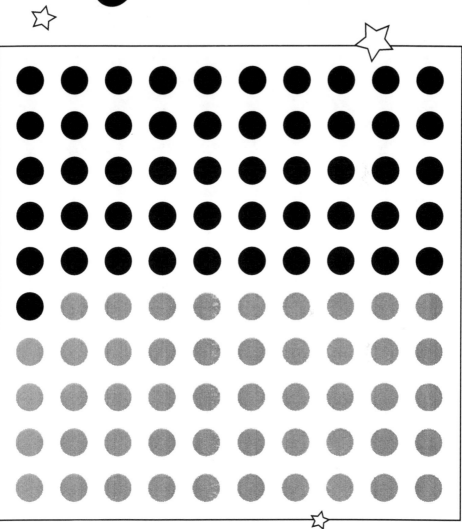

...or 51 Senators to be present. The Upper House of Senators can only begin a session if they have over fifty percent.

R stands for

Republic

...where elected officials represent you and me. This is an important aspect of our American democracy.

S stands for

Supreme Court

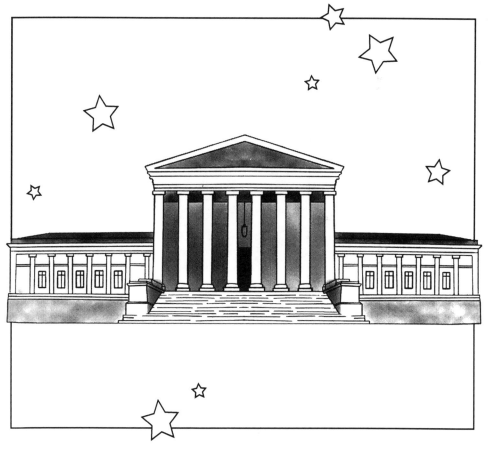

These 9 justices are appointed for life, and interpret the law, with the Constitution's support.

T stands for

Thirty Five

...stands for thirty five years old. This is the age you can run for President, an office you might someday hold.

U stands for

Unanimous

This is when everyone agrees on a decision, and can happen in our Supreme Court if all 9 justices see the decision as magnanimous.

V stands for

Veto

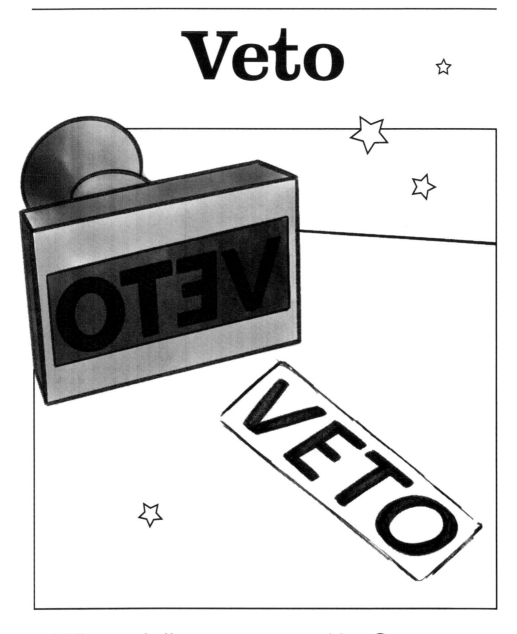

When a bill gets approved by Congress, the President can disapprove the law with a big "no."

W stands for

Washington, D.C.

Since 1790, this has been our
country's capital city.

X stands for

X (ten)

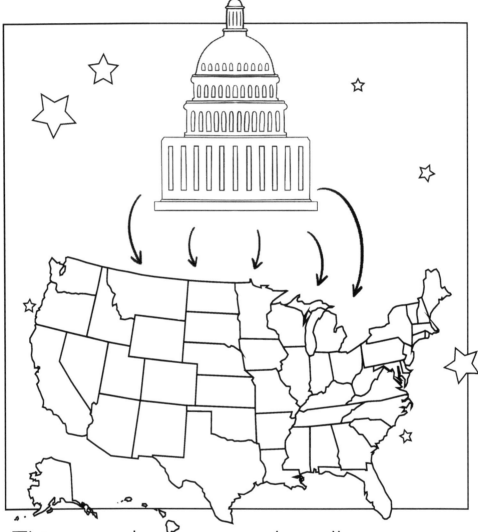

This amendment states that all powers not listed in the Constitution are returned to the states of women and men.

Y stands for

You

At 18, you become a voter, but before
then, your ideas and actions can
influence our government, too.

Z stands for

Zeal

This means enthusiasm to be
an active citizen, something
you and I can fulfill.

Want free goodies?!

Email us at

modernkidpress@gmail.com

Title the email "ABC Voter!" and we'll
send some goodies your way!

Follow us on
Instagram!
@modernkidpress

Questions: Email us at **modernkidpress@gmailcom!**